1/16

W9-CBR-348

EXCELLENT SCIENCE EXPERIMENTS

EXPERIMENTS WITH SOUND and LIGHT

Chris Oxlade
Consultant: John Farndon

PowerKiDS press

Published in 2015 by **The Rosen Publishing Group, Inc.**
29 East 21st Street, New York, NY 10010

Library of Congress Cataloging-in-Publication Data

Oxlade, Chris.
Experiments with sound and light / by Chris Oxlade.
p. cm. — (Excellent science experiments)
Includes index.
ISBN 978-1-4777-5966-0 (pbk.)
ISBN 978-1-4777-5967-7 (6-pack)
ISBN 978-1-4777-5965-3 (library binding)
1. Light — Experiments — Juvenile literature.
2. Sound — Experiments — Juvenile literature. I. Oxlade, Chris. II. Title.
QC360.O95 2015
535.078—d23

Publishing Director: Belinda Gallagher
Creative Director: Jo Cowan
Editors: Amanda Askew, Sarah Parkin
Editorial Assistant: Lauren White
Designers: Joe Jones, Kayleigh Allen
Cover Designer: Simon Lee

Photographer: Simon Pask
Production Manager: Elizabeth Collins
Reprographics: Stephan Davis, Thom Allaway,
  Anthony Cambray, Jennifer Hunt,
  Lorraine King

ACKNOWLEDGEMENTS
The publishers would like to thank the following sources for the use of their photographs:
Shutterstock.com Cover Ohn Mar; 6(tr) Ivan Cholakov Gostock-dot-net; 11(c) Yobidaba, (bl)
travis manley, (br) yalayama Fotolia.com Cover; 7(tr) Andres Rodriguez. Every effort has
been made to acknowledge the source and copyright holder of each picture. Miles Kelly
Publishing apologies for any unintentional errors or omissions.

Printed in the United States of America
CPSIA Compliance Information: Batch CWI5PK: For Further Information contact Rosen Publishing, New York, New York at 1-800-237-9932

CONTENTS

Learn all about light and sound, including how light travels and why we hear sounds.

Can you *see* sound? Find out on page 23.

Experiment time!

What happens when a light ray hits a mirror? Find out on page 13.

Help needed

Help and hazards

- All of the experiments are suitable for younger readers to conduct, but you will need help and supervision with some. This is usually because the experiment requires the use of scissors for cutting. These experiments are marked with a "Help needed" symbol.

- Read the instructions together with an adult before starting, and have an adult help to assemble the equipment and supervise the experiment.

- It may be useful for an adult to do a risk assessment to avoid any possible hazards before you begin. Check that long hair and any loose clothing are tied back.

- Check that sharp objects such as scissors are put away safely after use.

3

What is LIGHT?

Light is a type of energy that you can see. It is essential for all kinds of things. We need light to grow food and to be able to see around us. In earlier times, people used fires, candles, or oil for lighting. Now we make our own light with electricity or gas.

How light travels

Light travels in straight lines, called rays. Light rays change direction if they are reflected off or pass through an object or substance, but they still remain straight.

Hot light

Light is usually produced by a very hot object, such as a lightbulb or fire, and heat is released. The sun is our main source of light. Its rays travel through space and reach us as heat and light energy.

sun

Cold light

Some animals produce a kind of light that gives off no heat. Fireflies and glowworms are insects that can make parts of their bodies glow with light. About 1,500 different deep-sea fish give off light.

Viperfish

Refraction

When a straw is placed in water, it looks as though it is slightly bent. This is because light rays bend when they pass through water. This bending of rays is called refraction.

Reflection

When light hits a very smooth surface such as a mirror, it reflects (bounces) off the surface. If it hits a mirror at an angle, it is reflected off at exactly the same angle.

The eye receives a reflection of the image

Actual object

Light rays bounce off the mirror

4

What is SOUND?

Most sounds you hear, from the whisper of the wind to the roar of a jet, are actually moving air. Every sound originates with something vibrating. This makes the air vibrate too, and the vibrations in the air carry the sound to your ears. The vibrations that carry sound through the air are called sound waves.

Inside the ear

Tiny bones

Cochlea (fluid-filled chamber)

Outer ear

Eardrum

Ear canal

How do we hear sound?

The outer ear funnels sound waves into the ear. From there, sounds pass through a tube called the ear canal to the eardrum. Sounds make the eardrum and tiny bones in the middle ear vibrate. These bones pass the sound to the cochlea, in the inner ear, where nerve cells change the vibrations into messages that travel to the brain, which recognizes what we are hearing.

Sound measurement

The loudness (volume) of sound is measured in decibels (dB). A quiet sound, such as whispering, is 20 dB. A very loud sound, such as a jet plane taking off, is 120 dB.

Rustling leaves: 10 dB

Talking: 40 dB

Thunder: 100 dB

Atom bomb: 210 dB

Using this book

Each experiment has numbered instructions and clear explanations about your findings. Read through all the instructions before you start an experiment, and then follow them carefully, one at a time. If you are not sure what to do, ask an adult.

Introduction
See what you will be learning about in each experiment.

Things you will need
You should be able to find the equipment around the house or from a supermarket. No special equipment is needed. Always ask before using materials from home.

Safety
If there is a "Help needed" symbol at the start of the experiment, you must ask an adult to help you.

The warning symbol also tells you to be careful when using scissors. Always ask an adult for help.

Experiment symbols

① Shows how long the experiment will take once you have collected all the equipment you need.

② Shows if you need to ask an adult to help you with the experiment.

③ Shows how easy or difficult the experiment is to do.

① 15 min ② No help needed ③ Easy

BLOW some music

The clarinet, the trumpet, and the recorder are all instruments you blow to move the air and make a sound. Try this experiment to see how these wind instruments work.

You will need
• work surface
• square of card stock, 4 in. by 4 in.
• double-sided adhesive tape
• 20 drinking straws
• scissors

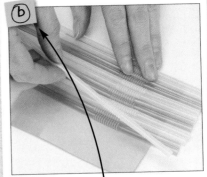

(a) Make sure the tape goes right to the edges

Put two strips of double-sided adhesive tape across the card stock at opposite edges. Remove the backing.

(b) With the tape at the top and bottom, press the straws onto the tape side by side. The ends of the straws must line up along the top of the card stock.

28

Stages
Numbers and letters guide you through the stages of each experiment.

Labels

Handy labels will provide you with useful tips and information to help your experiment run smoothly.

Explanation

At the end of each experiment is a question-and-answer explanation. It tells you what should have happened and why.

(Q) **What sounds do you make?**

(A) **The short straws produce higher notes than the long straws.** The straws work as tubes. When you blow across the top, the moving air creates vibrations that travel up and down each straw. The harder you blow, the stronger the vibrations grow, so the louder the sounds become. The short straws produce higher notes because the speed of the vibrations depends on the length of the tube – smaller tubes create faster vibrations.

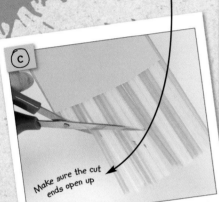

Make sure the cut ends open up

Diagonally cut off the bottoms of the straws. Cut across so that the first straw is about 4 inches long and the last straw is full length.

Also try...

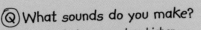

Fill glass bottles with different amounts of colored water. Blow across the tops of the bottles and listen to the different sounds you can make.

Also try...

Simple mini-experiments to test the science you've learned.

Hold the straw instrument with the tops of the straws near your bottom lip. Blow across the tops to produce sound.

29

Doing the experiments

✸ Clear a surface to work on, such as a table, and cover it with newspaper if you need to.

✸ You could wear an apron or old t-shirt to protect your clothing.

✸ Gather all the equipment you need before you start, and tidy up after each experiment.

✸ Ask an adult to help you when an experiment is marked with a "Help needed" or warning symbol.

✸ Work over a tray or sink when you are pouring water.

✸ Always ask an adult to help if you are unsure what to do.

Scientist KIT

Before you begin experimenting you will need to gather some equipment. You should be able to find all of it around the house or from a local supermarket. Ask an adult's permission before using anything and take care when you see a warning sign.

Flour

Handy hint!
Flour is messy! Make sure you do any experiments involving flour outside.

Foody things

- flour
- red, green, and blue food coloring
- sugar or salt

Handy hint!
Food coloring is very helpful because it allows you to see what is happening in your experiment and shows your results clearly.

Red Food Color

Food coloring

Card stock

From the Kitchen

- 3 clean, empty jars
- 20 drinking straws
- funnel
- glass or jar with a small opening
- jug
- scissors
- shallow plastic container
- small plate
- teaspoon
- water

Straws

Scissors

From the craft box

- adhesive tape
- card stock (white and colored)
- colored pencils
- double-sided adhesive tape
- large rubber bands
- modeling clay or sticky tack
- 2 pencils or pens, the same thickness
- pins
- short pencil
- stapler
- thick pen
- thin, white paper
- tracing paper

Pin

⚠ Warning!
Scissors are extremely sharp and can cut you easily. Make sure you ask an adult for help. When passing scissors, always point the handles towards the other person.

Pencils

Rubber bands

Other stuff

- balloons
- flashlight
- shoe boxes with lids
- small mirror

Mirror

Flashlight

Balloons

Places you'll need to work

- large outside space
- wall in a dark room
- work surface

Handy hint!
It doesn't have to be night-time to experiment in the dark. Just close your curtains and turn off any lights to create darkness.

Remember to recycle and reuse

One way to help the environment is by recycling and reusing materials such as glass, paper, plastics, and scrap metals. It is mostly cheaper and less wasteful than making new products from scratch.

Reusing means you use materials again in their original form rather than throwing them away.

Recycling is when materials are taken to a plant where they can be melted and remade into either the same or new products.

Handy hint!
Plastic bottles come in many different colors. Try to use a clear bottle so that you can see your experiment working.

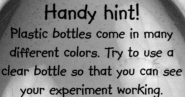

Hand SHADOWS

Shadows are made when something blocks light. Try this experiment to make shadows that are big or small, sharp or blurred.

15 min	No help needed	Easy

You will need
- wall in a dark room
- flashlight or lamp

Preparation

Turn off all the lights and shut the curtains, so the room is as dark as possible. Shine the flashlight on a wall. Either hold it or rest it on a level surface.

1a

Point your finger upwards and hold it about 2 inches in front of the flashlight's light.

1b

Watch the shape of the shadow →

Move your hand another 2 inches away from the flashlight.

Q What does the shadow look like?

A **It is large and blurred.** Your hand is close to the light source, so it blocks out a wide area of the light beam, making a large shadow. Having a wide light source like a flashlight close to your hand makes the edges of the shadow blurred.

10

Move your hand about 8 inches away from the flashlight.

Then move your hand as far away from the flashlight and as close to the wall as you can (without touching the wall).

Ⓠ How does the shadow change?

Ⓐ It becomes smaller and sharper. The further away your hand is from the light, the less of the beam your hand stops, so the smaller the shadow. The edges of the shadow are sharper because the light can't get around the edges of your hand.

Also try...

Put on a shadow puppet play. Make some puppets by cutting out card shapes, such as a horse or sheep. Then stick your puppet to a straw or short stick. Put these in front of the flashlight in the same way as you did with your hand. Start your "On the Farm" play! Use these shapes to help you.

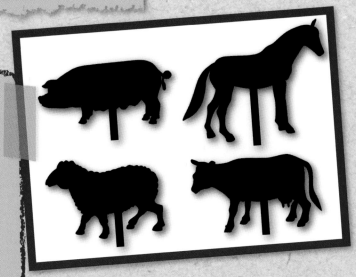

Ray of LIGHT

When you turn on a flashlight, it produces a ray of light. This experiment shows how light travels only in straight lines.

30 min • No help needed • Hard

You will need

- work surface
- 8.5 in. × 11 in. card stock (any color)
- scissors
- modeling clay or sticky tack
- flashlight
- small mirror

Preparation

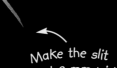

Make the slit about 2 mm wide

(a) Carefully cut a piece of card stock in half. Hold the pieces together and cut a slot 2 inches deep in one of the long edges.

(b) Stand one of the pieces of card stock on its slotted edge. Support it with four pieces of sticky tack or modeling clay near the corners.

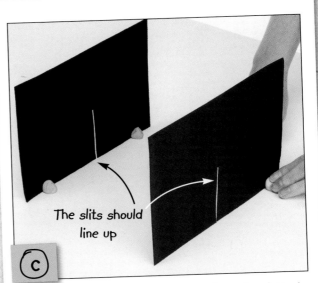

The slits should line up

(c) Stand the other piece of card stock on its slotted edge, parallel to the first piece and about 6 inches away from it. Support it with four pieces of modeling clay. The slots in the cards should be roughly opposite each other.

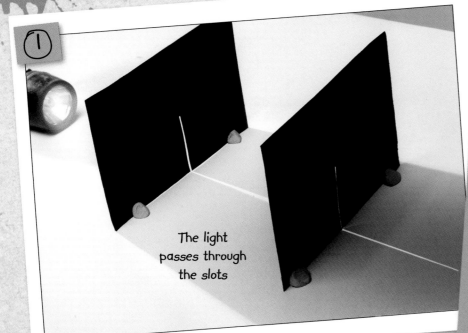

①

The light passes through the slots

Switch off the lights, or close the curtains to make the room dark. Shine a flashlight through one of the slots from about 4 inches away. Move the flashlight from side to side to make the ray pass through both slots.

Q What does the light do?

A The light ray passes through the slots. The light can only pass all the way through when the flashlight and both slots are all in line with each other. When the flashlight and slots are not in line, no light goes through the second slot. This shows that light travels only in straight lines.

②

Replace one piece of card stock with a mirror, with its reflecting side facing the remaining card. Shine the flashlight through the slot towards the mirror.

Bounce!

Q Does the light stop?

A No, the mirror reflects the light ray. The light ray that hits the mirror bounces back. When you move the flashlight from side to side, you'll see that the ray always bounces off the mirror at the same angle as it hits.

Through a LENS

In a camera, a glass or plastic lens bends light rays together to make an image that the camera records. Here's how to make a camera that makes a picture with just a simple hole.

30 min   Help needed   Hard

You will need

- work surface
- shoe box with lid
- scissors
- adhesive tape
- tracing paper
- flashlight
- colored card stock
- pin

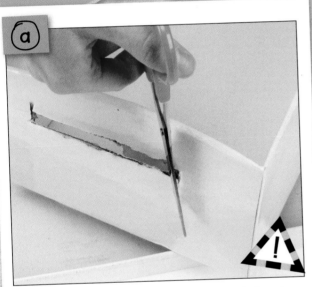

(a)

Carefully cut a hole about 3 inches by 2 inches in the center of one side of the box.

(b)

The tracing paper covers the large hole

Cut a piece of tracing paper about 4 inches by 2.5 inches. Stick it over the hole in the box, making sure it is not creased.

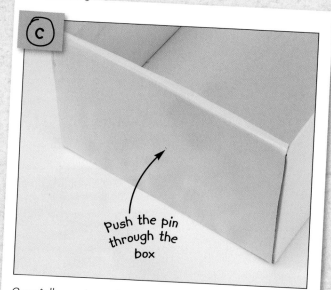

Carefully push a pin through the box, opposite the first hole, to make a small, round hole.

Turn off any lights and make the room as dark as possible. Hold the box in front of your face with the tracing paper screen closest to you. Aim the box at the flashlight. If the image is dim, try draping a cloth over your head and the top of the box.

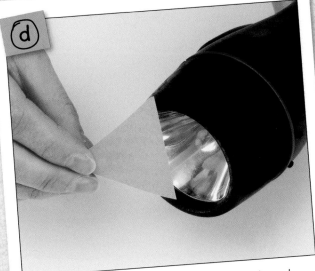

Cut a triangle shape in colored card stock and tape it to the front of the flashlight. Turn on the flashlight and rest it at head height.

Ⓠ What can you see?

Ⓐ **An upside-down triangle!** Rays of light coming from the flashlight go through the hole in the box and hit the screen. Light rays travel in straight lines, so rays traveling over the top of the triangle hit the bottom of the screen, and rays going under the bottom of the triangle hit the top of the screen.

Rainbow COLORS

A rainbow is made when sunlight splits into different colors. Here's how to make these rainbow colors.

15 min | Help needed | Hard

You will need

- work surface
- dark room
- shallow plastic container
- water
- jug
- small mirror
- sticky tack
- 8.5 in. x 11 in. card stock
- flashlight

(a) Rest a small mirror in one end of the container, angled at about 45 degrees, with the reflecting side facing upwards. Add a small piece of sticky tack to hold the mirror in place.

(b) Half fill the plastic container with water.

Rest the card against a glass or pile of books

(c) Balance a piece of card stock on the table at the other end of the plastic container.

(d) Make the room as dark as possible. Turn off the lights, close the curtains, and block any light coming into the room.

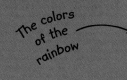
The colors of the rainbow

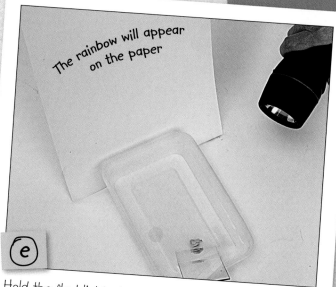
The rainbow will appear on the paper

(e) Hold the flashlight about 4 inches away from the mirror and turn it on. Make sure you shine the light on the mirror underneath the water. Adjust the angle of the flashlight until you see the colors of the rainbow on the card. What can you see?

Also try...

On a sunny day, stand with your back to the sun and spray water into the air in front of you. The sunlight is split into colors as it enters and exits the tiny drops of water in the air, making a rainbow.

(Q) Why can you see a rainbow?

(A) **Light from a flashlight and light from the sun is called white light.** It is made up of many different colors mixed together. The rays of light from the flashlight go into the water, bounce off the mirror, come out of the water again and hit the card stock. As the rays go in and out of the water they bend. The different colors bend by slightly different amounts, so they split up and you can see them. These colors are called the colors of the spectrum.

CHANGING colors

In these experiments, you can see how your eyes add colors, and how filters block out colors.

30 min

No help needed

Hard

You will need

- work surface
- white card stock
- small plate
- short pencil
- scissors
- water
- magneta (dark pink), cyan (blue/green) and yellow colored pencils
- 3 clean, empty jars
- red, green, and blue food coloring

1a

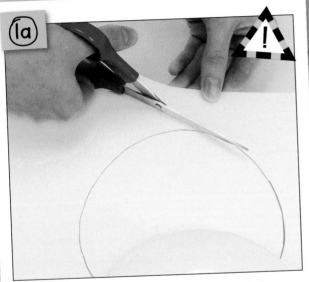

Draw around the small plate to make a circle on the card stock. Carefully cut out the circle.

1b

Make your colors strong

Draw lines to divide the circle into three equal sections. Color the sections magenta, cyan, and yellow.

1c

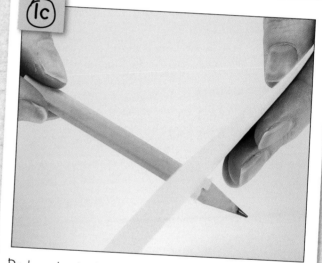

Push a short, sharp pencil through the center of the colored circle. Stand the pencil on its tip on a hard surface and then spin it.

Q Which color can you see?

A When you spin the spinner, your eyes merge the colors to make white or grey. By mixing cyan, magenta and yellow paints or colored pencils in different amounts, you can make any color you like. These special colors are called the primary colors of pigments.

18

Q Which two colors block light?

A Any two of red, green, and blue. These are the primary colors of light. The jars are filters. Each one lets through only one color of light (e.g. the red jar lets through only red light, and blocks green and blue). With two jars together, the color that goes through the first is blocked by the second (so green light from the green jar is blocked by the red jar).

Fill three jars with water. Add several drops of food coloring to each jar (red in one jar, blue in another jar, and green in the last jar).

2b Stand the green jar in front of the other two jars, with a window or other light source behind them. Look through the green jar. What do you see? Then try standing the red and blue jars in front.

Only green can be seen

Only red comes through

Only blue shows through

19

Picture flicker BOOK

Here's how to make an optical toy that shows how our eyes are fooled into seeing movement on a television or cinema screen.

30 min   No help needed   Easy

You will need

- work surface
- 12 or more small pieces of thin, white paper, about 4 in. by 3 in.
- stapler
- colored pens or pencils

(a)

Trace each image carefully

Draw a clock face on each of the pieces of paper. It must be in exactly the same place and look exactly the same, so trace each one.

(b)

Draw the hands on each clock face

On each piece of paper, change the time by one hour. You should have 12 o'clock, 1 o'clock, 2 o'clock, 3 o'clock, and so on.

c

The time should start at 12 o'clock and then move forward, hour by hour

Staple the pieces of paper together, making sure they are in the right order.

Also try... Try drawing more difficult images with more than 12 pieces of paper.

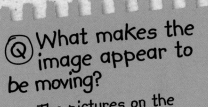

d

Now flick the pages from start to finish while watching the clock faces.

Q What makes the image appear to be moving?

A The pictures on the pages pass in front of your eyes one after the other, in quick succession, each for a split second. Your brain remembers each image for a short time, so you get the impression of a moving clock hand. Television and films work in the same way, showing images in quick succession on the screen.

Seeing SOUND

You can't actually *see* sound as it travels through the air. But here's an experiment that lets you see the vibrations that sound is made from.

15 min — No help needed — Easy

You will need

- work surface
- balloon
- scissors
- glass or jar with a small opening
- adhesive tape
- sugar or salt

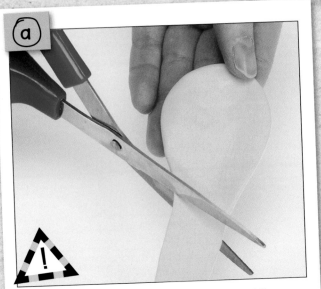

a

Carefully cut off the neck of a balloon and throw it away.

b

Your glass should have a small opening to fit the balloon over

Put the body of the balloon over the top of a glass. Stretch it to make a tight skin, like that on a drum.

22

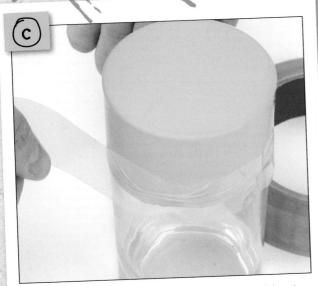

(c) Wrap some adhesive tape around the outside of the glass to keep the edge of the balloon in place.

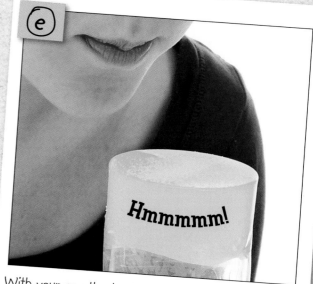

Hmmmmm!

(e) With your mouth about 4 inches from the balloon's surface, hum loudly. Also try humming a high note and a low note.

(d) Stand the glass on a table and put a few grains of salt or sugar on the balloon skin.

Q Do the grains on the balloon move?

A Yes! Sound is made up of vibrations that move through the air. The vibrations are called sound waves. When something makes a sound, vibrations spread out from it into the air in all directions. When the vibrations in the air hit something they make it vibrate, too. When sound waves from your mouth hit the stretched balloon, they make it vibrate up and down, which you can see because the grains jump up and down.

LIGHT
races sound

You hear sounds as soon as they are made. That's because sound travels really fast. Here's an experiment to prove it.

15 min

Help needed

Easy

You will need

- large outside space
- balloon
- flour
- funnel
- teaspoon
- pin
- helper

(a) Put the neck of a balloon over the funnel.

(b) Add the flour one spoonful at a time

Add a few spoonfuls of flour into the funnel and shake it down into the balloon.

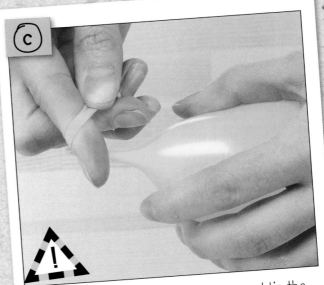

(c) Remove the funnel, inflate the balloon, and tie the neck to stop the air and flour from escaping. Don't inhale when blowing up the balloon – you'll get flour in your mouth.

(d)

Go outside to your large open space. Your helper should hold the balloon and a pin. Walk 100 large paces away from them.

(Q) **Which comes first, hearing the balloon pop or seeing the flour explode?**

(A) You should have seen the balloon burst, just before you heard the bang. This shows that light travels faster than sound. Light won the race easily. In fact, the difference in speeds is huge. Light travels at a staggering almost one billion feet per second – so fast that you see the balloon burst as it happens. Sound travels at just 1,116 feet per second. Its journey from the balloon will have taken just over half a second.

(e)

Ask your helper to hold the balloon away from their body. Look at the balloon and signal for your helper to pop it. Watch and listen very carefully – you will hear the balloon pop and see the flour escape.

Bang!

Musical BOX

The guitar and violin are both string instruments. Here's an experiment to see how strings make musical notes.

15 min | Help needed | Easy

You will need

- work surface
- shoe box with lid
- scissors
- 2 pencils or pens, the same thickness
- thick pen
- large rubber bands

Preparation

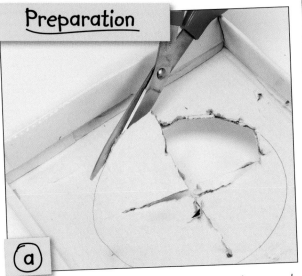

a

Cut a round hole about 6 inches across at one end of the box lid. Put the lid back on the box.

b

Stretch a few rubber bands lengthways around the box so that they run across the center of the hole.

c

The rubber bands must be tight

Put a pencil under the rubber bands at each end of the box. The pencils should lift the rubber bands clear of the hole.

Ping! Ping!

Pluck the rubber bands to make sounds. Pluck the bands hard to make loud sounds and softly to make quieter sounds.

①

Q Can you make sound?

A Yes because the rubber bands act as the string would on a guitar. When you pluck them, they vibrate from side to side. This vibrates the air around the strings, and you hear the vibrations as sound. The harder you pluck the strings, the stronger the vibrations are. Stronger vibrations make stronger sound waves, which sound louder. The box helps to make the sound louder because the sound bounces around inside it.

2b

Try moving the pen backwards and forwards to play different notes.

2a

Shorter length of rubber

Put a pen thicker than the pencils under the bands close to the hole. Pluck the bands again.

Q Does the sound get higher?

A Yes, because the pen changes the length of the rubber bands that can vibrate freely. The shorter this is, the faster the bands vibrate, and the higher the notes they make.

BLOW
some music

The clarinet, the trumpet, and the recorder are all instruments you blow to move the air and make a sound. Try this experiment to see how these wind instruments work.

You will need

- work surface
- square of card stock, 4 in. by 4 in.
- double-sided adhesive tape
- 20 drinking straws
- scissors

a Make sure the tape goes right to the edges

Put two strips of double-sided adhesive tape across the card stock at opposite edges. Remove the backing.

b With the tape at the top and bottom, press the straws onto the tape side by side. The ends of the straws must line up along the top of the card stock.

c

Make sure the cut ends open up

Diagonally cut off the bottoms of the straws. Cut across so that the first straw is about 4 inches long and the last straw is full length.

Q What sounds do you make?

A **The short straws produce higher notes than the long straws.** The straws work as tubes. When you blow across the top, the moving air creates vibrations that travel up and down each straw. The harder you blow, the stronger the vibrations grow, so the louder the sounds become. The short straws produce higher notes because the speed of the vibrations depends on the length of the tube – smaller tubes create faster vibrations.

Also try...

Fill glass bottles with different amounts of colored water. Blow across the tops of the bottles and listen to the different sounds you can make.

d

Hold the straw instrument with the tops of the straws near your bottom lip. Blow across the tops to produce sound.

Quiz ZONE

Get ready to test how much you've learned from the experiments in this book. Write down your answers on a piece of paper and then check them against the answers on page 31. No cheating!

check them against the answers on page 31.

QI picture clue

What are the missing words?

1. Shadows are made when _____ is blocked.

2. Smaller tubes create _____ vibrations than longer tubes.

3. The loudness (volume) of sound is measured in _____ .

4. Red, green and blue are known as the _____ colors of light.

5. Light from a flashlight and light from the sun is called _____ .

What word beginning with...

6. V carry sound to your ears?

7. R is made when white light splits into different colors?

Q7 picture clue

8. S is our main source of light?

9. R describes what a mirror does to a light ray?

30

True or false?

(10) Light rays always bounce off mirrors at different angles.

(11) Light travels only in straight lines.

QII picture clue

(12) Long straws produce higher notes than short straws.

Multiple choice

(13) If you blow into a straw and gradually increase how hard you blow, what will happen to the volume? It will get louder, it will stay same the same, or it will get quieter?

(14) Does sound travel really fast, really slowly, or not at all?

(15) Which would win in a race – light or sound?

(16) Light rays bend when they pass through water – is this called reflection, retention, or refraction?

Remember, remember

(17) What kind of light gives off no heat?

(18) How many feet does sound travel in a second?

Q19 picture clue

(19) Can we see sound?

(20) Which part of your body collects sounds in the air?

31

GLOSSARY

Angle The space between two straight lines or surfaces that join each other, usually measured in degrees.

Cold light A kind of light that gives off no heat.

Colors of the spectrum The rainbow colors you see when white light is broken up.

Decibel (dB) A unit for measuring the loudness (volume) of sound.

Filter A piece of equipment that allows only certain things to pass through it.

Hot light The light that is produced by a very hot object, such as the Sun. Heat is also released.

Inflate To fill something with air or gas so it becomes larger (expands).

Light rays The straight lines that light travels in.

Merge To combine or join things together to form one thing.

Optical Relating to machines or processes to do with light, images or the way we see things.

Primary colors of light Blue, green, and red are known as the primary colors of light.

Rainbow Made when white light splits into different colors.

Recycling When materials are taken to a plant where they can be melted and remade into either the same or new products.

Reflection When light hits a very smooth surface and bounces off it.

Refraction The bending of light rays when they pass through a substance, such as water.

Reusing Using materials again in their original form rather than throwing them away.

Shadow A dark patch on a surface that is produced when something blocks light.

Sound waves The vibrations in the air that carry sound to your ears.

Vibrate To move, or cause to move, a short distance quickly and continuously.

White light Light that is made up of many different colors mixed together, such as light from the Sun.

INDEX

WEBSITES

Due to the changing nature of Internet links, PowerKids Press has developed an online list of websites related to the subject of this book. This site is updated regularly. Please use this link to access the list:

www.powerkidslinks.com/ese/sound